Prayer

I0805380

Disciplines of Devotion

Edited by Winfree Brisley

Fasting, by Cassie Achermann

Prayer, by Courtney Reissig

Sabbath Rest, by Megan Hill

Prayer

Courtney Reissig

CROSSWAY®
WHEATON, ILLINOIS

Prayer

© 2026 by Courtney Reissig

Published by Crossway
1300 Crescent Street
Wheaton, Illinois 60187

All rights reserved. No part of this publication may be reproduced, stored in a retrieval system, or transmitted in any form by any means, electronic, mechanical, photocopy, recording, or otherwise, without the prior permission of the publisher, except as provided for by USA copyright law. Crossway® is a registered trademark in the United States of America.

Cover design: David Fassett

Cover image: Getty Images and Rawpixel

First printing 2026

Printed in the United States of America

Scripture quotations are from the ESV® Bible (The Holy Bible, English Standard Version®), © 2001 by Crossway, a publishing ministry of Good News Publishers. Used by permission. All rights reserved. The ESV text may not be quoted in any publication made available to the public by a Creative Commons license. The ESV may not be translated in whole or in part into any other language.

Trade paperback ISBN: 979-8-8749-0241-4
ePub ISBN: 979-8-8749-0243-8
PDF ISBN: 979-8-8749-0242-1

Library of Congress Cataloging-in-Publication Data

Names: Reissig, Courtney, 1983– author.
Title: Prayer / Courtney Reissig.
Description: Wheaton, Illinois : Crossway, 2026 | Series: Disciplines of devotion | Includes bibliographical references.
Identifiers: LCCN 2025004036 (print) | LCCN 2025004037 (ebook) | ISBN 9798874902414 (trade paperback) | ISBN 9798874902421 (pdf) | ISBN 9798874902438 (epub)
Subjects: LCSH: Prayer—Christianity. | Women—Religious life.
Classification: LCC BV210.3 .R457 2026 (print) | LCC BV210.3 (ebook) | DDC 248.3/2082—dc23/eng/20250825
LC record available at https://lccn.loc.gov/2025004036
LC ebook record available at https://lccn.loc.gov/2025004037

Crossway is a publishing ministry of Good News Publishers.

BP 35 34 33 32 31 30 29 28 27 26
15 14 13 12 11 10 9 8 7 6 5 4 3 2 1

Contents

Series Preface

ON A CHILLY JANUARY MORNING, two friends and I huddled around a coffee shop table to share life updates and prayer requests. One friend reflected on the previous year with frustration: "I feel like I didn't accomplish anything." The other friend and I, surprised by her assessment, rattled off a long list of worthwhile things she had done. But she persisted. It wasn't that she truly believed she had accomplished nothing; it was that the things she had done weren't the things she had hoped to do. Things she valued had been pushed aside by what seemed more urgent in the moment.

I could say the same, and I bet you could too. As women living in a do-it-all culture, we tend to have a lot on our plates. We juggle work, husbands, children, aging parents, and friends. We manage households, serve in the church, and volunteer in the community. Year after year, many of our goals and good intentions get pushed to the back burner—especially when it comes to spiritual growth.

We want to grow in relationship with the Lord. We want to know the Bible better, fight sin, and establish a consistent prayer life. But amid all the things we have to do, we often miss the one thing we really need. In Psalm 27:4 David said,

> One thing have I asked of the LORD,
>   that will I seek after:
> that I may dwell in the house of the LORD
>   all the days of my life,
> to gaze upon the beauty of the LORD
>   and to inquire in his temple.

As king, David surely had many things to do and many things he might have asked of God. But he knew that what he most needed was to dwell with the Lord. Similarly, Jesus explained to Martha in Luke 10:41–42 that she was "anxious and troubled about many things, but one thing is necessary." What was the one thing? Sitting at his feet, listening to his teaching.

As you consider your relationship with the Lord, are you more like David or Martha? Are you *devoted* or *distracted*? I suspect that many of us would admit that we identify with Martha's distraction but also long for David's devotion. So how can we grow in devotion to God in a world of endless distractions?

We see from both David and Martha that a life devoted to the Lord won't happen by accident. David resolved to seek after God's presence. Jesus suggested that Martha needed to sit down and listen. You see, discipline helps us grow in devotion.

In fact, throughout history Christians have used spiritual disciplines such as prayer, fasting, and Bible study to seek the Lord and grow in relationship with him. If the phrase "spiritual disciplines" sounds intimidating, don't worry! It simply means practices that promote spiritual growth.[1] And these practices can help you draw near to God whether you're a new believer or have been walking with the Lord for decades.

Perhaps the idea of cultivating a life of devotion to the Lord is new or confusing, and you don't know where to start. You have faith in Christ, but you're trying to figure out what it looks like to grow in relationship with him.

Or maybe you're going through the motions of spending time with God, but if you're honest, he feels distant. You want the Holy Spirit to warm your affections for the things of God and restore the joy of your salvation.

Or perhaps you have a vibrant relationship with the Lord, but you'd like to learn new ways to seek him. You've been wanting to try fasting or you'd like to learn about Sabbath rest.

Whatever your situation, the Disciplines of Devotion series was written for you. Each booklet explores

1 Donald S. Whitney, *Spiritual Disciplines for the Christian Life* (NavPress, 1991), 17.

one thing—one practice to cultivate, one spiritual discipline to grow in—to help you draw near to the one true God. In each booklet, you'll gain a biblical understanding of a particular discipline and why it's worth cultivating. And you'll explore three practical ways to get started.

If you'd like to grow in these disciplines alongside other believers, we've included reflection questions to facilitate group discussion. Consider using this series in one-on-one discipleship, with a group of teens, in a neighborhood Bible study, or with a church small group. Also, Christians have a variety of perspectives on these disciplines, so if you'd like to continue your personal study, you can find a list of recommended resources at the end of each booklet.

When you finish this volume, let me encourage you not to set it aside in a pile of good intentions. These booklets can be read in less than an hour, but the disciplines they recommend can help you seek the Lord for a lifetime—even as you go about all the things you have to do.

Preaching about the "one thing" David desired in Psalm 27:4, Scottish pastor Alexander Maclaren observed, "Most of us seem, to our own consciousness, to live amidst endless distractions all our days. . . . But if we are true to the one purpose of serving and keeping near God, then we have a charm against the frittering away of our lives in distractions."[2]

The Disciplines of Devotion series isn't about productivity or efficiency or doing less. It's about pursuing a life of devotion to the Lord in an age of endless distraction. It's an invitation to "taste and see that the LORD is good!" (Ps. 34:8) no matter how much is on your plate.

Winfree Brisley
SERIES EDITOR

2 Alexander Maclaren, *Expositions of Holy Scripture: Psalms* (Eerdmans, 1932), 146.

1

What Is Prayer?

PRAYER IS HARD FOR ME.

You may not have expected that to be the opening line of a resource on prayer. When we pick up books or resources on a topic, we typically want an expert opinion, tried-and-true tips, or something aspirational.

I'm not an expert, but of all the spiritual disciplines, prayer is the one I've seen God grow the most in my life in recent years. I've grown from someone who shrugged off my lack of fervor in prayer as "not my gift" to someone who looks forward to getting up early to pray—and praying all throughout the day.

God began this work in my life a few years ago when my pastor encouraged our church to make prayer a priority at the start of a new year. I usually dismissed such exhortations, seeing them as unattainable. *Prayer is not my thing*, I would tell myself. *We're all good at something when it comes to spiritual disciplines; prayer is not it for me.* But over time I couldn't shake a nagging conviction. God repeatedly exhorts us to pray in Scripture (Phil. 4:6; 1 Thess. 5:17; Heb. 4:16), so it wasn't something I could brush off as "not my thing."

If you struggle with prayer, let me assure you that you're not alone. I discuss the things that helped me later in the booklet, but for now, the point is this: While prayer might not come naturally to you, consistent prayer is not only possible but also necessary for your spiritual health.

For years, I wasn't willing to make changes for prayer to be a part of my daily life. But by God's grace, when my pastor challenged us, I was ready to seriously pursue growth in prayer. If you're at a similar crossroads with prayer, I hope this booklet shows you that it's possible. If I can grow in this discipline, you can too. And I hope you'll find, as I have, that prayer doesn't have to feel like duty or drudgery—it can be a means of delighting in the Lord.

Let's look at prayer together.

Defining Our Terms

Before we get too far, it's helpful to know what I mean when I'm talking about prayer. Tim Keller helpfully defines prayer as "a personal, communicative response to the knowledge of God." He adds, "Prayer is continuing a conversation that God has started through his Word and his grace, which eventually becomes a full encounter with him."[1]

At its core, prayer is talking to God. To understand why we talk to God through prayer, we need to go back to the beginning. We need to understand God's original intent for us as his created beings.

1 Timothy Keller, *Prayer: Experiencing Awe and Intimacy with God* (Penguin Books, 2016), 45, 48.

God created us for relationship with him. In Genesis, God walked in the garden he had made (Gen. 3:8). He talked to Adam and Eve (Gen. 1:28). But when Adam and Eve sinned, they could no longer be in God's presence (Gen. 3:22–24). And because we're sinful, we can't be in God's presence either. But God still wants a relationship with us. His desire to dwell among his people is the consistent story of Scripture from beginning to end.

In human relationships, what do you do when you want to have a relationship with someone but aren't with her in person? You talk to her. You interact through phone calls, letters, emails, and text messages, all the while planning opportunities to see each other in person.

There's a similar dynamic in our relationship with God. Right now we aren't with God. If we are in Christ, his Spirit indwells us, but we can't see him in the flesh. One day we will. One day Jesus will return, and God will dwell with his people forever in the new heaven and earth (Rev. 21:1–4). Prayer is how we can talk to God in the meantime. He has spoken to us in his word, and we speak to him in prayer. It helps us grow in relationship with him until we can be with him.

The Posture of Prayer

We have the opportunity to talk to God anytime, anywhere. He wants us to talk to him—he even commands us to talk to him—so why don't we? Why do we struggle to pray?

During Jesus's earthly ministry, people talked with him and came to him for healing and salvation. In a way, these men and women in the New Testament modeled prayer, how to talk to God.

Consider the father who brought his demon-possessed son to Jesus in Mark 9. This man came brokenhearted over his son. He was exhausted from saving his son from the demon's repeated attempts to harm him. First, he took his son to the disciples, but they couldn't cast the demon out. So he came to Jesus, and the scene was incredible. The demon was causing the son to convulse and foam at the mouth. The crowd grew around them, straining to see what was happening and what Jesus would do. And you can imagine the pain in this father's voice:

> "But if you can do anything, have compassion on us and help us." And Jesus said to him, " 'If you can'! All things are possible for one who believes." Immediately the father of the child cried out and said, "I believe; help my unbelief!" (Mark 9:22–24)

This father uttered only five words, but they are an example of the proper heart posture of prayer: "I believe; help my unbelief!" He didn't know exactly what to say, but he knew his need could be met only by Jesus. Only the desperate come to God for healing, salvation, and daily bread. You don't have to come with eloquent words, and you don't have to come with perfect faith. But you must know your need, or you will never come.

Making prayer a priority—a discipline—offers us a way to be daily reminded of our true condition. If you struggle to pray, take time to remember your need for God. Consider your dependence on God for every breath. Consider your sinfulness and the even greater grace of Christ. Come to Jesus like this father, and ask him to help your unbelief: *Lord, I believe prayer is important. I know I need you. Help my unbelief. Help me pray.*

How God Helps

Praying for God's help to pray may sound odd, but it's a prayer we can offer with confidence. God doesn't give any command that he doesn't also give the necessary grace to live out. He will help us pray. In fact, he already has in his word.

We find examples of prayer all over the Bible. In the Old Testament, Hannah prayed for a son when she went to the temple to sacrifice (1 Sam. 1:10), and she praised God in prayer when her request for a son was answered (1 Sam. 2:1–10). Solomon prayed for wisdom (1 Kings 3:9). The prophets prayed to God on behalf of God's people. And David wrote many psalms, which are prayers of lament, worship, repentance, and thanksgiving. He also praised God even when one of his prayers was not answered the way he asked (2 Sam. 12:15–23).

In the New Testament, we find many prayers that Paul wrote in his letters to the early church. And if there's ever a doubt that prayer is vital to healthy Christian discipleship, look no further than Jesus. He regularly withdrew from other demands to pray (Luke 5:15–16). He prayed early in the morning (Mark 1:35), and he prayed when he performed miracles (Matt. 14:19; Luke 9:16; John 11:41–42). He prayed not only in a time of deep emotional distress (Matt. 26:36–46) but also in the physical suffering of his crucifixion (Matt. 27:46; Mark 15:34; Luke 23:34, 46). Jesus truly prayed without ceasing. If Jesus needed consistent communication with his heavenly Father, so do we.

We can find help for how to pray in any of the recorded prayers in Scripture, but a good place to start is the prayer Jesus taught his disciples in Matthew 6:9–13, commonly called the Lord's Prayer:

> Our Father in heaven,
> hallowed be your name.
> Your kingdom come,

your will be done,
  on earth as it is in heaven.
Give us this day our daily bread,
and forgive us our debts,
  as we also have forgiven our debtors.
And lead us not into temptation,
  but deliver us from evil.

There's not one "right" way to pray, but in the Lord's Prayer, we find scaffolding for our prayers. When we pray, we come with many needs. The Lord's Prayer teaches us to make God the focus of our prayers and let all our requests flow from his work and character. We can boldly approach him as our Father as we also reverence his name. Praying for the furthering of his kingdom and the supremacy of his will before addressing our needs helps put our requests in the right perspective. Asking for daily bread and for forgiveness reminds us that God cares about and ultimately provides for both our physical and our spiritual needs. And we are reminded that we must extend forgiveness to others. Finally, praying for deliverance from evil reminds us that we must turn to the Lord and rely on him for resisting temptation.

I talk more about how to pray in the coming chapters, but for now remember this: God understands our weakness and our struggle with prayer. In Luke's Gospel, Jesus gave the Lord's Prayer after the disciples said, "Teach us to pray" (Luke 11:1). They admitted that prayer is hard—or that at a minimum they didn't know what to say. Jesus didn't rebuke them. Instead, he gave them words for their prayers. And he gave those words to help us too.

But Jesus does more than give us words we can pray. He is also praying for us (Rom. 8:34), and his Spirit is within us. Paul writes in Romans 8:26 that the Spirit "helps us in our weakness" because we don't always know what to pray. When we're at a loss, the Spirit is praying for us. When our words fail us, the Spirit never does. There isn't a prayer spoken (or left unspoken) that the Spirit doesn't guide and make complete by his power.

God expects us to talk to him because we're in a relationship with him. He wants us to bring our requests, offer praise, and confess our sins, but he doesn't leave us to figure it all out on our own. As we begin this journey of considering prayer together, let's make the disciples' request our prayer: "Lord, teach us to pray."

Reflection Questions

1. What has been your past experience with prayer (e.g., never tried it personally, done it inconsistently, have a thriving prayer life)?

2. What are some things that keep you from praying?

3. What are some things that motivate you to pray?

2

What Are the Blessings of Prayer?

A FEW YEARS AGO, a tornado came through our city. I'll never forget the desperate prayers of my children as we huddled under the stairs in our home for shelter—prayers like "God, please help us," "Please protect us," and "God, make the tornado move." I prayed too, begging God to keep us safe, and he did.

It's typically a given that we pray when a tornado is bearing down on our home and all we love. But the truth is, the dependence and need we face in those moments is ever before us, even when it is not tangibly felt. Prayer isn't just a lifeline when things fall apart. It's an opportunity to commune with God, to bring our needs before him, and to watch him work both in us and around us.

Why We Don't Pray

We're naturally self-sufficient. Many of us live in a modern society in which we have access to most everything at the push of a button on our phones. The immediacy of our needs being met dulls us to the reality that we have needs to begin with. Even when we do feel our needs more acutely, both our culture and our pride often demand that we avoid burdening others and instead hide our weaknesses and failures, putting on a brave face.

The reality of our dependence is a consistent theme throughout Scripture. From the time God breathed life into Adam's lungs until now, humanity has been dependent on God for every good thing in our lives including our daily sustenance (Luke 11:3), forgiveness of sins (Mark 2:7–11), salvation (Jonah

2:9; John 14:6), sanctification (1 Thess. 5:23), and even the continued existence of our world (Col. 1:17; Heb. 1:3). But our sin and limited understanding often prevent us from seeing these realities.

To highlight this truth, Jesus told his disciples in John 15:5 that apart from him they could do nothing. Jesus taught that he is the true vine and that his disciples are the branches. A branch brings nothing to its growth. It's dependent on the vine to nourish it to fruitfulness.

When we pray, we acknowledge something that's already true—we're dependent. Coming to the Lord with honesty and vulnerability can be hard for many reasons. If prayer is hard for you, one step may be to repent of your self-sufficiency. Another step may be to meditate on God's love for you as his child. There's freedom in admitting our faults and needs, as well as our doubts and fears. When we pray, we're admitting what's already true about us, and we're asking our gracious heavenly Father to meet us where we lack.

But maybe you hear this and think, *I know my need. That's why I can't pray.* Perhaps you're in the middle of a long illness, and your prayers have gone unanswered. Or you've lost a child, and the only things coming out of you are tears. Prayer feels like a cruel exercise in lost words. Pride and self-sufficiency often keep us from praying, but suffering has a way of making prayer seem impossible. If this is your story, be honest with God about it. Sit in the silence, weep, groan, or simply tell him that you don't know what to say, and then trust that the Spirit will meet you even there (Rom. 8:26).

Prayer Is Worth It

Even as I grow in understanding my dependence on God, prayer still isn't my natural impulse. When my feet hit the floor each morning, I think about all the things I need to do that day. I wonder if you do too. With so much on my mind, it's often much easier to start tackling my to-do list than to sit down, be still, and pray. That's why prayer is a spiritual discipline. Like a muscle, prayer must be trained. And the more consistently we pray, the easier it will eventually become. And when the brokenness of this world makes prayer a greater burden, the Spirit does the heavy lifting for us, groaning on our behalf until the words come out of our mouths.

It takes work to acknowledge our dependence, and it takes effort to engage our hearts and minds in prayer. But if we invest the time to cultivate this practice, we can experience some very real blessings. Let's consider some of the blessings of prayer.

Receiving Peace, Mercy, and Grace

Prayer is the avenue to bring our many burdens before the only one who can provide true relief. Paul tells the Philippian church, "Do not be anxious about anything, but in everything by prayer and supplication with thanksgiving let your requests be made known to God. And the peace of God, which surpasses all understanding, will guard your hearts and your minds in Christ Jesus" (Phil. 4:6–7). When we bring our requests to God, he gives us his peace and helps us trust him more. God cares about us. He wants us to be honest with him and cast our anxieties on him (1 Pet. 5:7). When we confess our sins, he gives us mercy and grace, and he cleanses us from our sin (Heb. 4:16; 1 John 1:9). The hymn "What a Friend We Have in Jesus" articulates this beautiful theology of prayer:

> What a friend we have in Jesus,
> All our sins and griefs to bear!
> What a privilege to carry
> Everything to God in prayer!
> O what peace we often forfeit,
> O what needless pain we bear,
> All because we do not carry
> Everything to God in prayer.[1]

Consider the imagery of giving God our burdens in prayer. If you've ever carried something heavy for any length of time, you know the relief that comes when you pass it off to someone else—or drop it on the ground. That's what happens when we take our burdens to God in prayer. We're instantly lighter. Whether

1 Joseph Medlicott Scriven, "What a Friend We Have in Jesus" (1855), https://www.hymnary.org/.

our barrier to prayer is pride or overwhelming grief, these are burdens he wants to take off our shoulders. And peace is waiting for us on the other side.

Shifting Our Perspective

Another blessing of prayer is that it shifts our perspective. As we depend on God for all things, we see his character and our need. Prayer orients our entire lives toward God and his purposes. We're moved into a posture of waiting on him to do what we can't. When we turn to God in our need, we see outside our own circumstances to a God who holds all things together (Heb. 1:3). In prayer, our gaze lifts up from ourselves to God.

One of my favorite examples of this sort of perspective shift is in 2 Kings 6:8–19. Elisha was a prophet who proclaimed God's word to the king of Israel. As the king of Syria bore down on Israel, he sought to eliminate all who stood against him, including Elisha. Elisha and his servant awoke one morning to an army encamped around them. His servant was in a panic, but Elisha was undeterred.

He told his servant, "Do not be afraid, for those who are with us are more than those who are with them" (v. 16). Elisha could have done a lot of things in that moment, but he did only one. He prayed: " 'O LORD, please open his eyes that he may see.' So the LORD opened the eyes of the young man, and he saw, and behold, the mountain was full of horses and chariots of fire all around Elisha" (v. 17).

Elisha continued to pray, asking God to strike the Syrians with blindness and to deliver him and his servant. Throughout this crisis, rather than looking anxiously at his dangerous circumstances, Elisha shifted his focus to God's faithfulness through prayer. But Elisha's dependence on God in prayer didn't just help Elisha, it also led to a perspective shift for his servant. Because of Elisha's prayer, the servant was able to see that the mountain was covered with the army of God.

We have the same benefit in prayer. When we turn from focusing on ourselves and our circumstances and cry out to God in prayer, our perspective shifts to behold God's glory and goodness. And as God answers our prayers for others, their perspectives can shift too.

Seeing God Work

This story also demonstrates another important blessing of prayer: We get to see God work as he answers. Elisha prayed for God to open the servant's eyes—and he did! Elisha prayed for God to strike the enemy army with blindness—and he did!

Isn't that amazing? Elisha made specific requests, and the Lord did what Elisha asked. Prayer isn't an empty ritual. As James 5:16 explains, "The prayer of a righteous person has great power as it is working." Of course, we must be careful to guard against coming to God as though he's a genie in a bottle, assuming he'll do whatever we ask. Sometimes he won't grant a specific request because, in his infinite wisdom, he knows it's not what's best. When it is not his will to grant a request, even if it is a good one, we grow by learning to simply trust him and his character. But the Lord really does move and act and work in response to his people's prayers. When we pray, we get to see God work.

Growing in Patience and Perseverance

God doesn't always answer us as quickly as he did Elisha. One hard reality of prayer is that we're often in a posture of waiting longer than we would like. The purpose of prayer is not to have all our prayers answered exactly when and how we want but instead to assume a posture of dependence and humble trust in God. We pray because we're in a relationship with God, and we know we need him to work in our lives and the lives of others. And as we wait on God, trusting him to answer, we find another blessing of prayer: growing in patience and perseverance.

John Newton is known for his many letters to weary Christians—often to dependent people waiting on God. In one of his letters, he says about prayer: "A patient waiting upon the Lord in prayer has often done wonders; for He is able to do more than we can ask or think."[2]

2 John Newton, "To Mrs. Ring: Letter III, On the Death of Mr. Cadogan," in *Letters of John Newton* (1869; repr. Banner of Truth, 2007), 409.

Zechariah and Elizabeth were two faithful believers who waited far longer than expected for God to answer their prayers. We see in Luke 1:6–7 that they were old and childless, though they were blameless before the Lord. What I love most about their story is how God went about answering Zechariah's prayer. One day while he was serving as a priest, Zechariah was chosen to offer prayers and incense to the Lord on behalf of the nation (vv. 8–9). As a righteous priest, he certainly offered prayers for Israel's deliverance, but notice what the angel Gabriel told him regarding his prayers: "Your prayer has been heard, and your wife Elizabeth will bear you a son" (v. 13). Zechariah had also been pouring out his heart before the Lord and sharing his personal longing to have a child, and Gabriel told him that Elizabeth would finally have a son. They had surely waited decades for God to answer this prayer, and in the middle of Zechariah's faithful labors as a priest, God sent his messenger to answer this prayer directly. Both Zechariah and Elizabeth persevered, continuing to lay their request before God, continuing to worship him, and patiently waiting on him to move. And in Zechariah's everyday obedience—faithfully serving as a priest—even though he doubted that God would indeed keep his word (v. 18–23), God did wonders. He provided the child who would one day prepare the way for the Son of God to begin his ministry (Mark 1:2–4).

God often does more than we even ask, because he works not only in the situation we're praying about but also in us as we wait. Paul explains in Romans 5:3–4 that "suffering produces endurance, and endurance produces character, and character produces hope." He also says in Romans 8:25 that "if we hope for what we do not see, we wait for it with patience." When God doesn't answer our prayers right away, we have the opportunity to grow in perseverance and patience.

When we fail to pray, we miss an opportunity for God to work in us and change us. We miss the chance to see him work and to be reminded of his goodness and care for us. And we miss the opportunity to grow in relationship with him. We need to pray because we need God. He invites us to acknowledge our need so that we can enjoy deeper communion with him, rest in his grace, and experience all the benefits of being in relationship with him.

Reflection Questions

1. Why do you think understanding our need for God is so important for prayer?

2. What are the things in your life that keep you from praying? Can you tell God about those things?

3. Can you think of a time when you knew you were dependent on God to act, and it led you to pray? What did you learn about God in that situation?

3

Pray Scripture

THE MOST FORMATIVE class I took in seminary was Personal Spiritual Disciplines with Donald Whitney. It was formative not only because he was a great teacher, but also because I was chronically late. Every day, he began class with prayer—praying a psalm, in fact. To select the psalm, he taught us a simple tool. Take the number of the day of the month, and add thirty a few times. For example, let's say it's the first of the month. You could pray Psalm 1, Psalm 31, Psalm 61, Psalm 91, or Psalm 121. Tardy students were called on to state the psalms of the day and then choose one to pray.

Suffice it to say, I got lots of practice praying the Psalms.

Dr. Whitney's rationale for teaching us to pray the Psalms has often come to mind in my struggles with prayer. He said we tend to "pray the same old things about the same old things."[1] I know this is true in my life, and I wonder if it is in yours as well. Have you ever begun praying, only to draw a blank just moments into it? You want to pray, but the words don't come. Or you make the same requests day after day after day. Maybe you lack direction or clarity.

If you don't want to pray the same things all the time, praying Scripture might be helpful. When we pray Scripture, whether it's a psalm or any other passage, we have fresh ideas to fuel our prayers each day. And it helps us ask for things according to God's will (1 John 5:14–15) because we're praying God's word back to him.

1 Donald S. Whitney, "How to Stop Praying the Same Old Things About the Same Old Things," Crossway, July 21, 2015, https://www.crossway.org/.

Pray the Psalms

Part of my daily rhythm of prayer includes praying a psalm. Christians have used this practice for centuries because many of the psalms are prayers. You can turn any verse or passage of Scripture into a prayer, but if you're familiar with the experience of trying to pray but drawing a blank on what to say, the book of Psalms is a good place to start.

In the previous chapter, I talked about how our prayers are often shaped by adversity. We pray in desperation but forget to pray in times of contentment. When we pray the Psalms though, we have a model for every context. We have psalms of celebration (Ps. 145), grief and lament (Ps. 88), deliverance (Ps. 34), confession of sin (Ps. 51), thanksgiving and praise (Ps. 92), and much more.

Here's what praying a psalm could look like. Turn to Psalm 22, a psalm that might be familiar to you because Jesus prayed it on the cross. You could pray this psalm about all sorts of situations, but as an example, imagine you want to pray for a friend who's suffering from cancer. Let's consider how you could pray this psalm for her. Verse 1 says:

> My God, my God, why have you forsaken me?
> Why are you so far from saving me, from the words of my groaning?

You could then pray like this: *God, it feels like you've forsaken my friend. As she walks through this journey with cancer, her cries have become groans. Why do you seem so far from her?*

Then move to verse 2:

> O my God, I cry by day, but you do not answer,
> and by night, but I find no rest.

When will relief come for her? Are her cries falling on deaf ears? Will you answer her as she cries out day and night? Will you answer me as I cry out for her day and night?

Sometimes we pray lament psalms and all we have are tears. When we are so stricken by grief that all we can do is cry, the Spirit hears even this and continues to intercede on our behalf (Rom. 8:26–27). But often, psalms give us words to pray and help us shift our prayers as our eyes are lifted to see God's character and promises. Look at Psalm 22:3–5:

> Yet you are holy,
> enthroned on the praises of Israel.
> In you our fathers trusted;
> they trusted, and you delivered them.
> To you they cried and were rescued;
> in you they trusted and were not put to shame.

God, you are holy, and I am not. You are perfect, and I am full of flaws. Yet you are a God who does not put me to shame. I stand in a long line of believers who have seen you work and found you worthy of trust. When I'm tempted to despair, let me remember that you were faithful to them, and you will be faithful to me and to my friend.

As we pray God's word, we're reminded of what he has done in the past, which fuels our faith for what he can and will do in the future.

Pray Any Scripture

Praying Scripture is not isolated to the Psalms or even the Old Testament. In the New Testament, Jesus frequently modeled prayer. The apostles also gave us words to pray. Nearly every one of the Epistles includes a rich prayer for the people to whom the apostles (such as Paul, James, or John) wrote. But we can also pray passages of Scripture that aren't specifically written as prayers.

A few years ago when I worked on a church staff, we went on a planning retreat for a day. The morning included a forty-five-minute block for individual prayer. At first, the idea felt overwhelming, but our pastor gave us a model for praying through Romans 8 and encouraged us to pray through its rich theology. While I initially thought the time would drag on, by the end I was frantically journaling, anxious for more time.

We started our time by reading the first verse of Romans 8. Our pastor prompted us to spend some time thinking and journaling about the verse, praying the words of the verse for people and situations that came to mind. We repeated the process for each verse that came after until we had a journal full of prayers for ourselves and others, all prompted by the words of Romans 8.

Because we will never fully mine the depths of Scripture, we will never run out of things to say to God when his own words guide us. As Whitney said, when we pray Scripture, we won't "pray the same old things about the same old things."[2] Allow God's word to shape and give language to your prayers.

Reflection Questions

1. How can praying Scripture make prayer easier for us?

2. What is a circumstance or person you want to pray for? How might using the Psalms or other Scripture passages help you pray for that situation?

2 Whitney, "Praying the Same Old Things."

4

Pray Purposefully

I'M A HIGH SCHOOL ENGLISH TEACHER, and if you know any teachers, you know that making lesson plans is a near-constant task. We're always thinking ahead to the next unit and building content around ideas and skills that we can continue teaching beyond one lesson. Some teachers may begin a year with no road map for where they're headed, preferring to make it up as they go along, but few succeed with this strategy. Effective teachers have purpose and direction.

The same is true for prayer. In Luke 11:1, the disciples asked Jesus, "Lord, teach us to pray." It's interesting that their request assumes prayer is something we need to learn how to do. They knew they needed a guide, and they knew where to go for help. As we saw in chapter 1, Jesus answered their request by giving them the Lord's Prayer as a model for what to say when we pray and the types of things we should pray for. But his personal habits in prayer also provided a model for the disciples—and for us.

Jesus regularly retreated to pray alone (Matt. 14:13, 23; Mark 6:46; Luke 5:16; 6:12; 9:18). He repeatedly removed himself from people and other distractions so he could have focused time with his heavenly Father. Jesus's example shows us that prayer doesn't happen accidentally. We must be purposeful in prayer.

In this chapter, we get really practical about the "how" of prayer. Different strategies will work for different people, but I want to show you practical ways I've found to be helpful in making my prayer time more intentional. The point is not for you to replicate what has worked for me but to find something that works for you.

As you read, you might pick one thing to try, and then see how God uses it. Commit to it for a period of time, and then evaluate whether it's helpful for you. If it's not, you might try another idea. As you work through this process, remember to be patient with the process of sanctification. Prayer is called a spiritual discipline for a reason, so don't be discouraged if it takes time to build prayer into a habit. The end goal of the Christian life is that we become more like Christ—all the way to glory. Only he prayed perfectly, but we can trust that he will finish what he started in us and help us grow (Phil. 1:6).

Make a Plan

When I prepared for a 10K race a few years ago, I found a running plan online and saved it in my phone. Every week, I knew what mileage I needed to run if I was going to finish the race. But I also had to take practical steps to follow the plan such as carving out time to go on all those runs and making sure I stayed hydrated.

The same is true in prayer. If we want prayer to be a regular practice in our lives, we need to start by making a plan. For example, I set a time of day for prayer, plan what requests I'll pray for, and assign a psalm to pray each day. I also plan to avoid distractions. For me, that involves planning where my phone will be when I pray and read my Bible—it needs to be nowhere near me! I pray in the morning, so I simply leave my phone on the charger until I finish reading my Bible and praying each day.

Use a Journal

The second part of my plan involves using a prayer journal. Some people use a prayer journal for writing out their prayers. I have good friends who have years of journals filled with written prayers. Not only does this method help you stay focused in prayer, but it also gives you a concrete record of the ways God has answered your prayers. It's a worthwhile practice to try.

I use a prayer journal in a different way. At the beginning of each month, I jot down people and situations I want to pray for. I use a journal that has categorized sections for my community, family, friends, church, heavy things (e.g., broken relationships, physical suffering, the things that keep me up at night), personal needs, and the world. (But you can choose your own categories.) Then I note which day of the week I'll pray for each category. This guides my prayers each day because I know going into Monday, for example, that I will always pray for missionaries in other countries (world), our local school district (community), our elected leaders (community), and my kids' teachers (community).

Set a Timer

I once heard an older woman say that to become more disciplined in prayer, she began setting a timer when she prayed. She was well into her sixties when she started this, and she began with five minutes at a time. This encouraged me that I could start a new habit too, so I followed her advice and began with five minutes. Every year, I added another minute. At the time of writing this booklet, I'm at eight minutes. At first, I was nervous I wouldn't be able to fill the time, but with a prayer journal guiding me and Scripture filling in words where I'm lacking, I find I often pray longer than the time allotted.

Pray Without Ceasing

We're wise to make plans that help us pray, but we also want to be careful about holding so tightly to allotted times and practices that we forget the Bible's exhortation to pray continuously (1 Thess. 5:17). In a moment of crisis, such as when a friend shares a need or you look at a dwindling bank account, you don't need to wait until your designated prayer time to pray. You can pray right then. Praying in the moment is also helpful if you, like so many other Christians, hear a friend's need and confidently say, "I'll be praying for you!" before inevitably forgetting about the request as soon as the conversation ends.

Praying spontaneously will come much more easily if your life is marked by prayer to begin with. As you pray purposefully with a plan, prayer increasingly marks your life—in scheduled and unscheduled times.

I love how Don Carson explains the need to pray purposefully in his book *A Call to Spiritual Reformation*:

> This is the fundamental reason why set times for prayer are important: they ensure that vague desires for prayer are concretized in regular practice. . . . [T]he fact remains that unless we plan to pray we will not pray. The reason we pray so little is that we do not plan to pray. Wise planning will ensure that we devote ourselves to prayer often, even if for brief periods: it is better to pray often with brevity than rarely but at great length. But the worst option is simply not to pray—and that will be the controlling pattern unless we plan to pray. If we intend to change our habits, we must start here.[1]

Jesus assumes we will pray, and the disciples assume we will need help. Perhaps Carson's encouragement is the help you need today—start by planning to pray.

1 D. A. Carson, *A Call to Spiritual Reformation: Priorities from Paul and His Prayers* (Baker Academic, 2000), 20.

Reflection Questions

1. What can we learn from Jesus's habits with prayer? How was his approach different from yours?

2. What is one practical suggestion from this chapter that seems helpful to you? How could you begin to implement it in your life?

5

Pray with Others

I LED A WOMEN'S Bible study in my living room every Thursday night for several years. I loved gathering with other women around God's word, but what I loved most was how we ended each gathering. We divided into smaller groups, shared prayer requests, and prayed together. I still remember nights spent praying for lost family members, financial needs, empty wombs, physical and emotional suffering, and anything else these sisters carried with them into my home on Thursday nights.

Praying together bonded us. There were women who were young, old, and everywhere in between, and we all learned from each other. We learned how to carry burdens, and we learned how to pray.

As we wrap up this booklet, it's important to highlight the corporate aspects of prayer. In a Western society, we're prone to an individualistic mindset, even when it comes to our spiritual lives. It's true that our faith must be personal, but God calls individuals to be part of his corporate people—the church. He adopts us as his children into a family that extends beyond our bloodlines with mothers, fathers, sisters, and brothers. As a family, we cry out to our Father together. As we intercede for one another and bear each other's burdens, we grow in relationship with God and with each other. And we grow in prayer because we learn by practice and by example. We are able to hear how others pray, and we get the opportunity to practice praying. We see the faith of fellow believers modeled in their prayers, and we gain greater confidence in our own prayers.

Four Ways to Pray with Others

I want to acknowledge that praying out loud can be quite fearful for some. If that's you, please know that you can be a faithful Christian and never pray out loud in church. My hope with offering these examples of how to pray with others is that you will find one you can implement or even one you can begin praying about implementing.

Pray with Children

Children are forgiving, which is why I begin with this one. They don't have a lot of specific expectations about how prayer should go, so you can relax and not worry about saying exactly the right thing. If you don't have children of your own, you probably have opportunities to interact with nieces and nephews, your friends' children, or kids at church. As you spend time with family and friends or serve in the nursery or children's Sunday school, practice praying out loud with the kids.

If you're a parent, you're the first model of prayer for your kids, but it doesn't have to be elaborate. Praying together can be as simple as praying before meals, praying before bed, or praying on the way to school. Then build toward asking your kids for prayer requests and praying about those together. I've included resources at the end of this booklet that can give you guidance on what to pray with your kids, but even using some of the suggestions in this booklet as a family (such as praying a psalm every day) is a great start.

Even as you yourself are learning to pray, teaching children to pray is a wonderful form of discipleship. You get to model for them what it looks like to learn a spiritual discipline, even as a grown-up.

Pray with Your Spouse or Roommate

Few things bond you to people like praying with them. Praying with your spouse or roommate gives you a window into the other person's needs and allows you to share your burdens.

If you're married, it can be as simple as beginning each day or ending each night in prayer together for a few minutes. Share one way you can specifically pray for each other, and build from there. The most important thing is that you find a time that works and stick to it. You might even put it on the calendar if that helps you stay consistent.

If you aren't married but have a roommate, you can apply this principle in your relationship with her. I know a single woman who gathers weekly with her roommates to pray. They share prayer requests, pray for each other, and pray for needs at their church—such as missionaries or people on the church prayer list.

Pray with Friends

When my children began school, I joined a group of moms who gathered weekly to pray for our school and teachers. I learned about the needs of our school, but I also grew in prayer as I learned how to pray from other moms. I heard their struggles and how they cried out to God.

Praying with close friends also gives us opportunities to come alongside those struggling with sin. When we confess our sins to one another, we find accountability, help in resisting temptation, and the ability to walk in the light with fellow believers (James 5:16; 1 John 1:6–7). Praying with friends about our sin can be a significant tool for our sanctification.

Similarly, you could pray with friends by gathering people around a specific need or interest. One woman I know hosted prayer and listening nights in the aftermath of shootings of unarmed Black men across the United States. Women would meet to lament injustice and suffering, listen to the experiences of others, and pray for healing in our country. You might gather to pray with friends in your workplace during lunch or ask friends in your neighborhood to join you on prayer walks. You could even take advantage of technology and set a regular time to pray with a friend who lives far away using Zoom or FaceTime.

Pray with the Church

The New Testament church gathered regularly to pray (Acts 2:42), and to this day, God's people gather to pray at weekly and monthly prayer meetings all over the world. The church prayer gathering is a beautiful thing that has stood the test of time.

While I don't currently attend a church that has a weekly prayer gathering (we have periodic meetings throughout the year), I have the sweetest memories of Wednesday night prayer at my church in seminary. In those weekly meetings, I heard Scripture-saturated and faith-filled prayers from people desperate for God to save lost family members, provide a building for our young church plant, and even meet the needs of missionaries we supported. I heard needs I would never have known about, and then watched other believers step in to pray for those needs. And I saw God answer the cries of his people.

If your church has a weekly prayer meeting and you aren't in the habit of going, I encourage you to attend. If your church doesn't have dedicated prayer meetings, consider other church activities that would give you the opportunity to pray with fellow church members. Perhaps there are small groups or women's Bible studies that incorporate times of prayer.

Bound Together in Prayer

The Christian life is not for lone rangers. We're members of one body with one heavenly Father. We are also called to bear one another's burdens (Gal. 6:2;

James 5:16), and praying for our needs together allows us to be vulnerable with God and with trusted brothers and sisters. As we grow in our discipline of prayer, praying with others is an integral part of the process.

Reflection Questions

1. What is your experience with praying with others? Are there people you could ask to begin praying with regularly? Is there a corporate prayer time you could join at your church?

2. What is one thing from this booklet that has changed the way you think about prayer?

3. What is one thing from this booklet that you would like to put into regular practice?

Conclusion

THE GOAL OF THIS booklet is to show, from one struggling pray-er to another, that prayer is possible and is valuable to our spiritual growth. But maybe you've gotten to the end of this booklet, and you still have questions.

Perhaps you prefer spontaneity. Or you come from a background of legalism and you're hesitant about prescribed practices. Maybe all this planning seems to take the joy, the relationship, and the Holy Spirit out of prayer. These are valid concerns. We must always be careful that we don't slide into believing that our actions earn our salvation or end up doing something as an empty ritual.

God desires a relationship with us, and prayer is a means of communication in that relationship. We certainly don't want to forget that the goal of everything in this booklet is for us to draw near to God, to dwell in his presence. But even our most connected relationships take effort and planning on our part.

As I write this conclusion, my family is beginning the holiday season, one of the busiest times of year. If we don't plan intentional time together, it won't happen. Of course, we'll still be a family even if we don't have dedicated quality time, but we'll miss out on the relational connection of being together and enjoying each other.

The same is true in our relationship with the Lord. There's nothing we can do to earn our place in his family or to lose it once we're saved by grace through faith, but we do need to put forth effort in our relationship with God in order to grow. Because we love our heavenly Father, we want to spend time with him and be like him. And because we are his children, he wants to hear from us in prayer.

If we remember that prayer is a discipline, then we also remember that discipline takes effort. All good athletes work at their sport. All skilled musicians practice their instrument. Discipline requires denial of one thing for the advancement of another. Prayer must both be learned and practiced. Jesus teaches us to pray, and the Holy Spirit helps us pray. But if we want to get better at prayer, we have to just do it.

As you think about what step you want to take in pursuing greater discipline in prayer, I want to return to the running metaphor. We're all running a race that ends when we're with our Savior in glory (Heb. 12:1). And we all need prayer to help us grow in relationship with the Lord in the meantime.

But the things that have helped me grow in prayer might not all work for you. Maybe there's one thing I mentioned that you want to try, or something I said that sparked a new idea I didn't even mention. Pray and ask the Holy Spirit to bring to mind something you can do to grow in prayer—and do that! The point is to do something. Preparing for a race takes planning and strategy, but at some point you have to go out and start running. So pick a starting point with prayer, and then run toward the Lord with all your heart.

Recommended Resources

Carson, D. A. *Praying with Paul: A Call to Spiritual Reformation*. Baker Academic, 2015.

This is my favorite book on prayer. D. A. Carson walks through the New Testament model of prayer using the many instances where Paul prays in his epistles. Along the way, he also gives a biblical treatment to our deep need for prayer. If you want to do a deep dive into New Testament prayer and find additional models for praying Scripture, this is your book.

Hill, Megan. *Praying Together: The Priority and Privilege of Prayer in Our Homes, Communities, and Churches*. Crossway, 2016.

Along with praying purposefully, the Bible assumes we will pray with others. As you grow in the discipline of prayer, you need others to walk alongside you. Megan Hill's book provides a rationale and gives helpful models for praying with other people.

Keller, Timothy. *Prayer: Experiencing Awe and Intimacy with God*. Penguin Books, 2016.

This book is both theological and practical. Tim Keller is rich in his understanding of why we pray, but he also models how to pray. If you're left wanting to understand a deeper model for prayer, this is a good place to start.

Laferton, Carl, ed. *5 Things to Pray*. 10 vols. (unnumbered). Good Book, 2016–2024.

We all need models for prayer, and this series guides you through praying for particular things (children, spouse, parents, etc.) with specific prompts drawn from Scripture.

Whitney, Donald S. *Praying the Bible*. Crossway, 2015.

If you want more language for your prayers, Donald Whitney gives deeper models for praying Scripture, particularly the Psalms. This is a great companion as you grow in prayer.

TGC THE GOSPEL COALITION

The Gospel Coalition (TGC) exists to renew and unify the contemporary church in the ancient gospel by declaring, defending, and applying the good news of Jesus to all of life.

Guided by a Council of more than 40 pastors in the Reformed tradition, TGC seeks to foster a mighty movement of spiritual renewal. We want to see God bless local churches with a gospel-centered ministry that fully integrates corporate worship, expository preaching, joyful obedience to God's Word, effective evangelism, loving community, and faithful engagement in the world.

Through its women's initiatives, TGC aims to equip, connect, and encourage women's ministry leaders and women in local churches globally. We do this through in-person gatherings and by producing resources including Bible studies, articles, podcasts, cohorts, books, and curricula. We support the growth of women in faithfully studying and sharing the Scriptures, in actively loving and serving the church, and in spreading the gospel of Jesus Christ in all their callings.

Join us by visiting TGC.org so you can be equipped to love God with all your heart, soul, mind, and strength, and to love your neighbor as yourself.

TGC.org

The Disciplines of Devotion Series

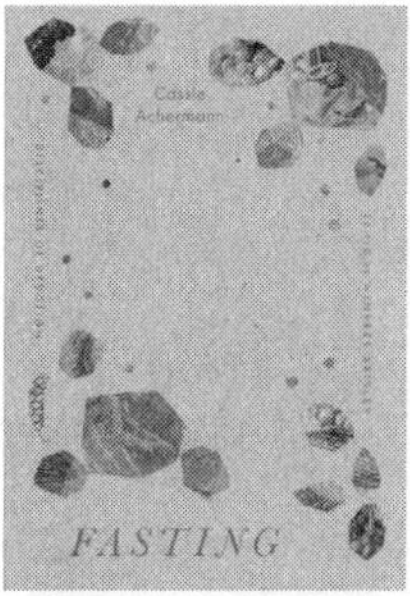

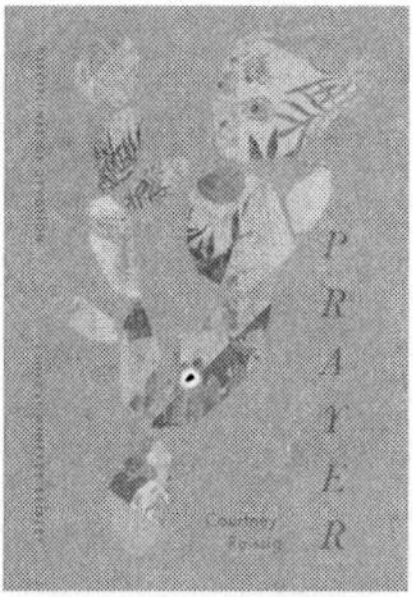

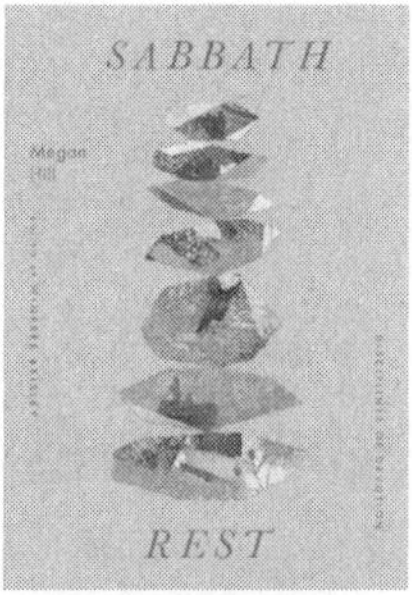

For more information, visit **crossway.org**.

"The Disciplines of Devotion series is a timely and valuable resource for women who long to grow in spiritual depth and maturity. With biblical insight and godly wisdom, each volume offers practical help for cultivating habits that lead us closer to Christ. I'm thankful for this series and eager to see how God will use it to strengthen and encourage the hearts of women."

Melissa B. Kruger, author; Vice President of Discipleship Programming, The Gospel Coalition

"These gospel-centered primers are saturated with scriptures that nourish the delight of knowing Christ. The accessible content, coupled with practical ideas and heart-oriented application questions, invites the reader to draw near to God through cultivating Spirit-empowered holy habits."

Karen Hodge, Coordinator of Women's Ministries, Presbyterian Church in America; coauthor, *Transformed: Life-Taker to Life-Giver* and *Life-Giving Leadership*